GUINNESS W★RLD RECORDS

RECORD-BREAKING COMPREHENSION

The RED book

Gill Howell

Published by

RISING ★ STARS

in association with

Rising Stars UK Ltd.
7 Hatchers Mews, Bermondsey Street, London, SE1 3GS
www.risingstars-uk.com

Published 2013
Reprinted 2013

Published in association with Guinness World Records.

Author: Gill Howell
Text design: Burville-Riley Partnership/Fakenham Prepress Solutions
Logo design: Words & Pictures Ltd
Typesetting: Fakenham Prepress Solutions
Cover design: Burville-Riley Partnership
Publisher: Becca Law
Project manager: Tracey Cowell
Editor: Jennie Clifford

Photo acknowledgements
Page 8: © © Kazuhiko Yoshino/iStockphoto; **pages 8 and 9**: © Kita Telles/iStockphoto; **page 10**: © John Carnemolla/iStockphoto; **pages 10 and 11**: © Gary Martin/iStockphoto; **pages 12 and 13**: © Moonshadow Media/iStockphoto; **page 14**: © Yegor Tsyba/iStockphoto; **page 18**: © Pink Moustache/Vector Stories; **page 22**: © Moral Medya/iStockphoto **page 28**: © A-R-T/shutterstock; **pages 32 and 33**: © Digoarpi/iStockphoto; **pages 36 and 37**: © Yegor Tsyba/iStockphoto; **page 40**: © Tribalium/iStockphoto; **page 42**: © Exxorian/iStockphoto; **pages 44 and 45**: © Antagain/ iStockphoto; **page 46**: © Kazuhiko Yoshino/iStockphoto (spiral notebook), © PHOTOgraphica/ iStockphoto (pen); **pages 46 and 47**: © YinYang/iStockphoto; **page 52**: © Grafissimo/iStockphoto. **Rising Stars is grateful to Guinness World Records for supplying all of the record-related pictures in the book.**

British Library Cataloguing in Publication Data.
A CIP record for this book is available from the British Library.

ISBN: 978-0-85769-564-2

Printed by Craft Print International Limited, Singapore

CONTENTS

HOW TO USE THIS BOOK

Record-Breaking Comprehension features some of the most fascinating, weird and wonderful records from the Guinness World Records archive.

In this book, you will:

- read the exciting record-breaking stories
- practise and improve your comprehension skills
- go beyond the record to find out more.

The text

Each record or topic is described using a fiction or non-fiction text type, including newspaper reports, instructional web pages, blog entries and letters.

RECORD-BREAKING COMPREHENSION

MOST EXPENSIVE PAINTING BY ELEPHANTS

Jo's travel diary

19 February 2005
Chiang Mai, Thailand

Wow! An amazing day today! I've just come back from the Maesa Elephant Camp near Chiang Mai.

I was expecting to help the staff wash the elephants, and maybe even ride on one, but when I arrived I found the elephants were attempting a Guinness World Record for painting! So, in the end, I spent the day watching animals creating art instead.

There were eight elephant artists (yes, real elephants), all doing real painting. It was fascinating. They held the paintbrushes with their trunks and took short breaks every hour. It took them six hours to finish painting two canvases. Afterwards, the elephants' canvases were joined together to form one big painting.

The finished painting was called *Cold Wind, Swirling Mist, Charming Lanna I* and was bought by Ms Panit Warin, a Thai woman who lives in California, USA. She paid 1.5 million baht for it. That's more than £20,000! It was the most expensive painting by elephants ever.

She donated one half of the painting to the Thai Government and let the Elephant Camp keep the other half for display in the camp's own gallery.

The elephants seemed to really like painting. I just wish I could afford to buy one too!

Questions

Answer the questions to help you practise and improve your reading comprehension skills.

For help on answering questions, see pages 6–7.

The questions cover a range of different reading skills. For more information on these skills, see page 56.

Most expensive painting by elephants

ON YOUR MARKS

a. Where did Jo visit on 19 February 2005?

b. In what way was Jo's day 'amazing'?

c. Why do you think Ms Panit Warin let the camp have one half of the painting in their gallery?

GET SET

a. Where is the elephant camp?

b. Why do you think the elephants needed to take short breaks?

c. What record was achieved at the camp?

GO FOR GOLD!

a. What happened after the elephants had finished painting the two canvases?

b. How did Jo feel about not being able to wash or ride the elephants?

c. Why do you think Jo wished she could afford to buy one of the paintings?

Beyond the record

In this section you will be asked to find out more about a record or topic and present your findings. This might be by using books or the internet.

BEYOND THE RECORD

What do you think the purpose of the elephant camp is? Discuss with a partner and then make a list of all your ideas.

9

READING COMPREHENSION

Reading the text

Read the text carefully. Don't rush. Try to immerse yourself in the information and enjoy it.

When you have finished, take a moment to reflect and think about what you have read. What was the author's purpose? Did the text make sense? Was there anything you didn't understand?

The questions

Always read the questions carefully before you begin to write. Then you will understand what you are being asked to do.

The questions check that you can:

- make sense of what you are reading
- find information and ideas in the text
- work out what the author means
- understand why a text is organised in a particular way
- comment on vocabulary and style
- say how a text makes you feel
- link what you read to your own life.

Answering the questions

Read the instructions carefully before you start to answer, as they give you information about how to answer the questions. Don't rush your answer.

Remember to refer to the text. You do not need to answer any questions from memory.

READING BETWEEN THE LINES

An author doesn't always tell you exactly what is happening. He or she often gives you clues to help you work it out for yourself.

Read the text below and then look at the worked question examples underneath.

Woofs and wags abounded at the annual Summer Fair. There were 15 entrants who competed for the Toss and Fetch Cup. This was won by Andy May and Buster. Buster caught one disc as many times as Andy could throw it in 60 seconds. He gained extra points by making several mid-air catches and was awarded a respectable 9.5 points.

Another duo, Misty and Olivia, hope to go on to international competitions.

'We are practising hard to get Misty holding more discs and want to try for the Guinness World Record,' said proud owner Olivia.

a. How many entrants were in the competition?

The answer can be found in the text itself – 15.

b. What or who is Buster?

The text doesn't actually say, but from reading the clues ('Woofs and wags', 'Toss and Fetch Cup') it becomes clear that Buster is a dog.

c. How did Misty's owner feel about her dog's success?

Again, the text doesn't actually say, but you can draw your own conclusion from the text: '"We are practising hard to get Misty holding more discs and want to try for the Guinness World Record," said proud owner Olivia' implies that Olivia is very pleased with Misty's success.

MOST EXPENSIVE PAINTING BY ELEPHANTS

Jo's travel diary

**19 February 2005
Chiang Mai, Thailand**

Wow! An amazing day today! I've just come back from the Maesa Elephant Camp near Chiang Mai.

I was expecting to help the staff wash the elephants, and maybe even ride on one, but when I arrived I found the elephants were attempting a Guinness World Record for painting! So, in the end, I spent the day watching animals creating art instead.

There were eight elephant artists (yes, real elephants), all doing real painting. It was fascinating. They held the paintbrushes with their trunks and took short breaks every hour. It took them six hours to finish painting two canvases. Afterwards, the elephants' canvases were joined together to form one big painting.

The finished painting was called *Cold Wind, Swirling Mist, Charming Lanna I* and was bought by Ms Panit Warin, a Thai woman who lives in California, USA. She paid 1.5 million baht for it. That's more than £20,000! It was the most expensive painting by elephants ever.

She donated one half of the painting to the Thai Government and let the Elephant Camp keep the other half for display in the camp's own gallery.

The elephants seemed to really like painting. I just wish I could afford to buy one too!

ON YOUR MARKS

a. Where did Jo visit on 19 February 2005?

b. In what way was Jo's day 'amazing'?

c. Why do you think Ms Panit Warin let the camp have one half of the painting in their gallery?

GET SET

a. Where is the elephant camp?

b. Why do you think the elephants needed to take short breaks?

c. What record was achieved at the camp?

GO FOR GOLD!

a. What happened after the elephants had finished painting the two canvases?

b. How did Jo feel about not being able to wash or ride the elephants?

c. Why do you think Jo wished she could afford to buy one of the paintings?

BEYOND THE RECORD

What do you think the purpose of the elephant camp is? Discuss with a partner and then make a list of all your ideas.

Encyclopedia of animals

Birds

Ostriches

Ostriches live in the wild in Africa, but they are also kept on farms for their feathers, eggs and meat in many other parts of the world, including the UK.

Did you know?

- Ostriches lay the largest eggs of any living bird.
- Ostriches are the tallest and heaviest birds in the world. An ostrich can reach 2.7 m in height and weigh 159 kg.
- Ostriches do not fly – they run! An ostrich can run at 40 miles an hour. That is a faster land speed than any other bird.
- An ostrich eye is almost 5 cm across – the largest eye of any land animal.

Record-breaking egg

The largest egg on record was laid by an ostrich on 17 May 2008 at a farm in Sweden owned by Kerstin and Gunnar Sahlin.

An average ostrich egg weighs around 1.5 kg, but this giant egg weighed 2.589 kg. One large chicken egg weighs about 57 g. That means the weight of this ostrich egg was about the same as 45 chicken eggs. That's a very big omelette!

135

ON YOUR MARKS

a. Where was the largest ostrich egg laid?

b. Can any other bird run faster than an ostrich?

c. How do you think the Sahlins felt when they first saw the egg?

GET SET

a. How fast can an ostrich run?

b. When do you think an ostrich would need to run fast?

c. Why do you think bullet points are used?

GO FOR GOLD!

a. Where do you find wild ostriches?

b. Why do you think ostrich eggs are bigger than chicken eggs?

c. Why does the author compare the ostrich egg with chicken eggs?

BEYOND THE RECORD

Imagine you are a poultry farmer who has decided to start farming ostriches. How might an ostrich farm be different from an ordinary poultry farm? What special requirements might it need?

Aerial feats

ACROBATICS

Cirque du Soleil (meaning 'circus of the sun' in French) began in Canada in 1984. It started as a group of stilt-walking entertainers. Since then, Cirque du Soleil has entertained people from all over the world with acrobatic displays that defy gravity.

Cirque du Soleil performers need a range of skills and talents. They must have grace, strength and be fearless.

Brandon Pereyda is a 28-year-old aerialist from Las Vegas, USA. Brandon was excellent at gymnastics when he was at high school, and was the only boy invited to join the cheerleading team. After leaving school, Brandon began teaching himself to do aerial stunts.

In June 2007, Brandon appeared on *America's Got Talent*. The audience loved him, but the judges thought he needed more practice.

Brandon was spotted on television by members of Cirque du Soleil and was offered an audition. Since then, he has starred in many of their performances. Brandon has broken the Guinness World Record for the most rotations on a vertical rope in one minute, achieving 13 rotations. He broke the record in Cologne, Germany on 23 November 2007.

ON YOUR MARKS

a. In which country did Cirque du Soleil begin?

b. Where does Brandon Pereyda work?

c. Was Brandon a success on *America's Got Talent*?

GET SET

a. Which city does Brandon Pereyda come from?

b. Why was it unusual for Brandon to join the school cheerleading team?

c. Why do you think Brandon appeared on *America's Got Talent*?

GO FOR GOLD!

a. What does 'Cirque du Soleil' mean in English?

b. What does the author mean by 'defy gravity'?

c. Why do you think Brandon attempted a Guinness World Record?

BEYOND THE RECORD

Imagine you are advertising the Cirque du Soleil. Find out more about the circus on the internet. What information would you use to convince people to visit?

THE STORY OF KING MIDAS

King Midas was a foolish king who loved gold above everything else. One day, in his garden, he saw an old servant of the god Dionysus. He took in the servant and treated him so well that Dionysus wanted to grant King Midas a wish.

King Midas said, 'I want everything I touch to turn to gold.' So Dionysus granted the wish.

At first, Midas was pleased to see gold appear when he touched things, but then he touched his food, and it turned to gold. He grew hungry and thin. His horse turned to gold, his servants ran from him, and even his daughter became a golden statue.

Midas realised how foolish he had been and begged Dionysus to take the wish away.

So be careful what you wish for!

80 cm

Did you know...?

- Gold is often seen as a symbol of goodness or great achievement. This is where the phrase 'golden touch' comes from. People who own a lot of gold are said to be successful.

- The largest gold coin in the world weighs 1,012 kg and measures 80 cm in diameter and 13 cm in thickness. The coin was introduced on 9 February 2012 by the Perth Mint (Australia).

ON YOUR MARKS

a. Who did King Midas see in his garden?

b. Why did King Midas grow hungry and thin?

c. What kind of text is the story of King Midas?

GET SET

a. What does gold symbolise?

b. Why did King Midas's servants run away from him?

c. Why did King Midas think he had been foolish?

GO FOR GOLD!

a. What is the thickness of the largest gold coin?

b. What do you think 'So be careful what you wish for!' means?

c. What does the author want you to think after reading the story?

BEYOND THE RECORD

Think about the phrase 'golden touch'. Use two different sources, for example a website and a book, to find other phrases that use the word 'gold'. How many can you find?

Try something new at the Webworth Festival!

A unicycle is a one-wheeled cycle without handlebars or gears. You can't coast on a unicycle but must keep pedalling. This means you will develop stronger stomach and leg muscles and better balance than people who ride ordinary bicycles.

Though growing in popularity, the unicycle is still an unusual type of transport, and people will be amazed, fascinated and curious when they see you speeding by.

You'll never run out of challenges on a unicycle.

How about:

- riding backwards, or with one foot?
- mountain unicycling or freestyle unicycling?
- the ultimate wheel unicycle, which doesn't have a seat?
- the Giraffe unicycle, which has a seat that's at least 1.52 m high?

Try setting a record!

Some people have become Guinness World Record holders as unicyclists.

Sam Wakeling and Roger Davies from the UK broke the Guinness World Record for the fastest journey from Land's End to John O'Groats by unicycle.
It took them 6 days, 8 hours, 43 minutes from 12–19 September 2009.

TWO WHEELS OR ONE? GET A UNICYCLE AND YOU'LL SOON SEE ONE WHEEL IS GREAT!

ON YOUR MARKS

a. How many wheels does a unicycle have?

b. What can you do on a bicycle that you cannot do on a unicycle?

c. Why might people look at you on a unicycle?

GET SET

a. What must the rider keep doing on a unicycle?

b. Why does the author describe bicycles as 'ordinary'?

c. What challenge would you face when riding the ultimate wheel unicycle?

GO FOR GOLD!

a. Where did Sam Wakeling and Roger Davies cycle to achieve a Guinness World Record?

b. What effect might unicycling have on your fitness?

c. How does the author of this text feel about unicycling?

BEYOND THE RECORD

Use two sources to find out about bicycles through the ages. Write a historical report about bicycles. Think about how you will present your information. You could present it as a Mind Map™ or timeline.

Moustache fact file

Definition: Facial hair grown on the upper lip

Word origin: From the Ancient Greek word 'mustax', meaning upper lip

Common abbreviations: tache, tash, mo

Oldest known moustache image: A moustached nomadic horseman was painted in about 300 BC

Famous moustaches: *The Dalí*

A narrow moustache with sharp outer points that curve upwards. It was named after the artist Salvador Dalí.

The Fu Manchu

A narrow moustache with very long points that fall below the chin. It was named after a fictional Chinese character.

The Horseshoe

A wide and long moustache growing around and down the sides of the mouth to the base of the jaw.

The Toothbrush

This moustache covers the centre of the upper lip with straight sides. The most famous toothbrush moustache was worn by Adolf Hitler.

On 4 March 2010, Ram Singh Chauhan (India) broke the Guinness World Record for the longest moustache. It measured 4.29 m on the set of *Lo Show dei Record** in Rome, Italy.

**Lo Show dei Record*: An Italian Guinness World Records TV show.

Encyclopedia of the Human Body **29**

ON YOUR MARKS

a. What is a moustache?

b. How do we know people wore moustaches in ancient times?

c. Why is Ram Singh Chauhan famous for his moustache?

GET SET

a. Where does the term 'moustache' come from?

b. Which type of moustache was made famous by a story?

c. Which moustache was named after a real person?

GO FOR GOLD!

a. Which country does the man with the longest moustache come from?

b. Why do you think the horseshoe moustache has this name?

c. Do you need to read the information in the fact file from top to bottom? Why?

BEYOND THE RECORD

Look again at the information about famous moustaches. Create a poster to explain what each moustache looks like, using headings, artwork and labels. Swap your work with a partner – can you guess which moustache is which?

www.bogsnorkellinguk.com

Bog snorkelling

Bog snorkelling was invented in 1976 by a group of friends and, since then, has attracted competitors from all over the world. Entrants must swim two lengths of a 55m trench cut into a peat bog. The trench is full of water, mud and weeds.

The rules of bog snorkelling are simple:
- Normal swimming strokes are not allowed; only flipper power must be used.
- Entrants must use a snorkel and mask.

The World Bog Snorkelling Triathlon

The World Bog Snorkelling Triathlon is an annual event that began in 2005. It takes place in Llanwrtyd Wells, Wales. Competitors start by running 12 km, followed by two lengths of a peat bog trench, before finally cycling 31 km across the Welsh countryside.

Record-breaking Bent

In 2010, the winner of the event was Daniel Bent from Surrey. He also became a Guinness World Record holder for the fastest time to complete the World Bog Snorkelling Triathlon. He completed the course in 2 hours, 23 minutes, 24 seconds on 11 July. This was the second time Daniel had won the event.

Daniel has had a taste for adventure all his life. When he was four, he decided to cycle down the steps of his home. The cuts, bruises and sore head didn't stop him from wanting more. As well as bog snorkelling, Daniel has completed a 9,000-mile charity bike ride from England to India.

ON YOUR MARKS

a. How long is a bog-snorkelling trench?

b. What do you think might be difficult about swimming in a peat bog trench?

c. What happened to Daniel when he cycled down the steps of his home?

GET SET

a. What three events make up the World Bog Snorkelling Triathlon?

b. Why did Daniel Bent cycle to India?

c. Which part of the triathlon do you think is most difficult. Why?

GO FOR GOLD!

a. In what year did the World Bog Snorkelling Triathlon start?

b. What event started Daniel Bent's desire for adventure?

c. Why do you think the World Bog Snorkelling Triathlon attracts competitors from all over the world?

BEYOND THE RECORD

Use three different websites to research other unusual sports, such as cheese rolling, pancake racing or welly throwing. Use your findings to create an alphabetised information sheet.

Balloon power

Helium-filled party balloons can be great fun. Helium is a 'lighter-than-air' gas, so when balloons are filled with it they float.

Some things can be lifted from the ground when they are tied to enough helium balloons, even people. This is known as cluster ballooning.

However, unlike hot-air balloons, the only way to control the 'flight' is to pop the balloons, or let go of some of them.

On 4 August 2001, Mike Howard (UK) and Steve Davis (USA) broke the Guinness World Record for the highest altitude reached by helium-filled party balloons. They reached a height of 5,577.85 m using 1,400 helium-filled balloons near Albuquerque in New Mexico, USA. Both Steve and Mike are experienced balloonists and pilots.

In the photo above, Steve and Mike are sitting on a simple gondola under the balloons.

Don't try this at home!

Larry Walters got himself into trouble when cluster ballooning. In 1982, he attached 42 helium balloons to a garden chair he was sitting on. He only wanted to rise about 100 m off the ground but instead rose rapidly to 5,000 m and drifted into restricted airspace. Eventually, he shot some of the balloons with a pellet gun. He was arrested by police when he landed.

Yoshikazu Suzuki, a piano tuner from Japan, wanted to float across the Pacific Ocean to the USA, powered by 26 helium balloons. He took off and was spotted two days later, but then was never seen again.

ON YOUR MARKS

a. What is helium?

b. What do you think happened to Yoshikazu Suzuki?

c. Why do you think the sub-heading says 'Don't try this at home!'?

GET SET

a. Who got arrested after his cluster-balloon flight?

b. What do you think 'restricted airspace' means?

c. What happened when Larry Walters used his pellet gun?

GO FOR GOLD!

a. Where did Yoshikazu Suzuki want to go?

b. Why is controlling a cluster of helium-filled balloons difficult?

c. What helped to make Mike and Steve's balloon flight a success?

BEYOND THE RECORD

Imagine you are planning a cluster-balloon flight attempt. What could you do to make the attempt safer? Think about what you might do before the flight and what you would take with you on the flight.

MOST DISC CASES TOPPLED IN A DOMINO FASHION

www.activitiesforkidzathome.com/dominotoppling

How to ... | **Domino Day** | **Types of dominoes** | **History** | **Toppling**

Chain reaction

Have you ever tried setting up dominoes, one after the other, and knocking them over? This is called domino toppling.

Rules

There are two basic rules for domino toppling.

1. The 'pushover' must start from one place.
2. Once the chain reaction ends, the attempt is over. Only the number of dominoes that fall over can be counted.

Domino toppling tips and tricks

- To make sure your dominoes stand in a perfectly straight line, use a ruler and draw a line before placing the dominoes.
- In hard-to-reach places, use a pair of tweezers to place the dominoes so you don't knock them accidentally with your hand.
- To create interesting effects, use different-coloured dominoes, or paint the reverse in different colours. As the dominoes topple, the colours will appear.
- The size and weight of the dominoes is important. Different types and sizes of dominoes will topple at different speeds.
- Toppling dominoes in different patterns is more difficult – and therefore more exciting. Try zig-zag patterns or spirals.

Don't have dominoes? Why not try toppling disc cases instead, like Tim Weißker?

Tim broke the Guinness World Record for the most disc cases toppled in a domino fashion. He toppled a whopping 5,969 disc cases at Dientzenhofer-Gymnasium in Bamberg, Germany, on 12 September 2011.

ON YOUR MARKS

a. Which Guinness World Record did Tim Weißker break?

b. How would drawing a line help you set up dominoes?

c. How could accidentally knocking a domino with your hand affect a toppling attempt?

GET SET

a. What is domino toppling?

b. Why is the size of the dominoes important?

c. What is a 'chain reaction'?

GO FOR GOLD!

a. How many disc cases did Tim Weißker topple on 12 September 2011?

b. In what way are zig-zags and spirals more exciting than straight lines?

c. What effect could you get by using dominoes of different weights and sizes?

BEYOND THE RECORD

How could you present the information in this web page to someone younger, to explain the rules and tips of domino toppling? Think about the use of headings, colour and images.

LONGEST TIME TO SPIN A BASKETBALL ON THE HEAD

Spinning a basketball on the head or finger

To spin a basketball on your finger, follow these instructions and you will soon be amazing your friends!

1. First, toss up the ball, twisting your hands to make it spin, then catch it. Try to twist the ball faster each time.
2. Next, make sure the ball is spinning straight. If it is spinning at an angle, you can't balance it on your finger.
3. Practise spinning the ball fast and straight, then try catching it on your fingertip. This works best with your finger slightly bent. If your finger is totally straight, the ball will just bounce off.

If you practise, practise, practise, you might get as good as Mehmet Kekec from Germany. He spun a basketball on his head for 18.11 seconds and broke the Guinness World Record for the longest duration spinning a basketball on the head. He had to spin the basketball on his finger first before transferring it to his head. Mehmet broke the record at the Soccer Meets Schanze charity event in Hamburg, Germany, on 28 May 2011.

Tips

- Balance the ball on your fingernail. It has less friction than your fingertip. Less friction means a faster spin.
- Toss the ball high enough so that you can see the middle of the bottom of the ball. This helps you judge where the right spot is to put your finger.
- Fan (lightly brush) the ball with the fingertips of your other hand. This will make it spin faster.

ON YOUR MARKS

a. How do you make the basketball spin when you start?

b. What happens if you balance the ball on your fingernail?

c. Why does the author write the word 'practise' three times?

GET SET

a. What happens if the ball is spinning at an angle?

b. What effect does friction have?

c. Where is the 'right spot' for spinning a basketball?

GO FOR GOLD!

a. Why should your finger be bent when you catch the basketball?

b. Why does the author use the word 'might' in the final paragraph?

c. Why do you think Mehmet Kekec spun the ball on his finger first?

BEYOND THE RECORD

Imagine Mehmet Kekec is coming to visit your school. What five questions would you like to ask him? If you could ask only one question, what would it be?

LARGEST HUMAN CHRISTMAS TREE

All over the world, people decorate their homes at Christmas with a Christmas tree. **6**

Christmas trees became popular in Britain when Queen Victoria and her husband, Prince Albert, began to decorate their home with a real fir tree at Christmas. **14**

There is a legend that the first Christmas trees began as symbols of Christmas in Germany about one thousand years ago, when a monk from Devon went to convert people to Christianity. **24**

The Georgian kings brought the Christmas tree from Germany to Britain but, because the kings were unpopular, it didn't catch on with the public.

In the 1960s, silver Christmas trees made from aluminium were introduced. These needed little or no extra decoration. **1**

Today, artificial Christmas trees look very like the real thing: some even have in-built lights. **3**

One tree you would not want in your house is the largest human Christmas tree. The tree was made up of 672 people and was created at an event organised by a business called E-Plus Gruppe on 8 December 2011 in Dusseldorf, Germany. **20**

When Queen Victoria died, the Christmas tree tradition died out. However, after World War I people needed something to celebrate, so the Christmas tree became popular again. Poorer people had small trees made from feathers or brush fibres. **18**

COUNTDOWN TO CHRISTMAS

ON YOUR MARKS

a. Who introduced Christmas trees to Germany?

b. Why might having in-built lights be an advantage in an artificial tree?

c. Why did aluminium trees need little or no decoration?

GET SET

a. What type of trees are used as Christmas trees?

b. After World War I, why did poorer people have small feather or brush Christmas trees?

c. Why wouldn't you want the human Christmas tree in your house?

GO FOR GOLD!

a. Who brought Christmas trees from Germany to Britain?

b. Why do you think Queen Victoria and Prince Albert made Christmas trees popular?

c. Why do you think 672 people wanted to be part of the largest human Christmas tree Guinness World Record?

BEYOND THE RECORD

Use three different sources to find out about Christmas tree farms and sustainability. Use the information you find to write a list of advantages and disadvantages of buying a real fir tree for Christmas.

YOUNGEST SWORD SWALLOWER

Sword tricks

SWORD SWALLOWING

You may think that sword swallowing is a modern invention but it has, in fact, been around for thousands of years.

2000 BC	It is generally accepted that sword swallowing originated in India. Holy men used the practice to show their power.
1st century AD	Sword swallowing was taken up in Ancient Greece and Rome.
8th century AD	In Japan, sword swallowing became part of a form of acrobatic theatre called Sangaku.
The Middle Ages	Medieval street performers made sword swallowing more popular in Europe.
19th century AD	Sword swallowing as entertainment began to die out.
1893	In Scandinavia, the practice of sword swallowing was outlawed. However, in the same year, it was featured at the Chicago World Fair and sword swallowing became popular in the USA.
2002	The Sword Swallowers Association International (SSAI) was launched. It was set up to preserve the art of sword swallowing for both amateurs and professionals around the world.
2006	The last Saturday of each February was proclaimed annual 'World Sword Swallower's Day' by the SSAI to promote worldwide appreciation for this unique and extremely dangerous art.

DO NOT TRY THIS AT HOME!
Never try to swallow a sword. It can take years to learn this performance art and it is **very** dangerous.

The youngest recorded sword swallower in the world is Erik Kloeker, who swallowed a solid steel sword, up to the hilt, at the age of 16 years, 267 days, on 21 July 2006.

52 *Circus Skills*

ON YOUR MARKS

a. In which country did sword swallowing begin?

b. What does 'outlawed' mean?

c. Why does the author describe sword swallowing as 'extremely dangerous'?

GET SET

a. What is Sangaku?

b. Why do you think sword swallowing was outlawed in Scandinavia?

c. What is the difference between amateur and professional sword swallowers?

GO FOR GOLD!

a. When did sword swallowing become more popular in Europe?

b. Do you think sword swallowing is difficult? Why?

c. How do you think forming an association would preserve the practice of sword swallowing?

BEYOND THE RECORD

Design a persuasive poster to advertise a sword-swallowing event at a festival. Use four powerful adjectives to encourage people to attend.

The Royal Exchange Theatre

Presents

A night of music with L. Athira Krishna

L. Athira Krishna is a gifted violinist who was born in 1987 in Kerala, India. As part of a musical family, she began playing the violin at the age of eight and first performed in public at the age of nine. When she was 12, she started touring all over the world.

During her incredible career, Athira has won many awards, including 16 international and six national awards. Her musical abilities earned her the title 'Musical Gem of India', an award that was presented to her by the First Lady of India.

Athira also broke a Guinness World Record for a 32-hour-long non-stop violin concert, which was dedicated to global peace and harmony. This marathon performance took place over 10–11 November 2003, at the Soorya Dance and Music Festival, Trivandrum, Kerala, India. Athira was only 16 at the time.

Although she first trained in Indian classical music, Athira has also studied Western classical music and has developed a style of her own, which blends different cultural styles.

Athira believes strongly in the healing power of music and has held music therapy sessions for hospital patients in Kerala and Chennai. Athira's future plans involve using music to help people of the world, and to create a new musical style with global appeal.

ON YOUR MARKS

a. How old was Athira when she began performing in public concerts?

b. What does Athira believe music can do for people?

c. How do you think being born into a musical family influenced Athira?

GET SET

a. How many international and national awards has Athira won?

b. What do you think Athira hoped to achieve when she played non-stop for 32 hours?

c. What does 'blends different cultural styles' mean?

GO FOR GOLD!

a. What sort of music did Athira first train in?

b. Why does the author say 'Athira was only 16 at the time'?

c. Why do you think the award is called 'Musical Gem of India'?

BEYOND THE RECORD

Plan a concert to be held in school. Who would you ask to perform and who would attend? What would you need to do to make your concert a success? Think about the best way to organise your ideas: headings and bulleted lists, or a spider diagram?

www.pavementart.com/home

HOME / ABOUT / CONTACT US

PAVEMENT ART

Pavement artists are called 'screevers'. They draw pictures on pavements using coloured chalk, and often put down a cap to collect money from passers-by. The word 'screever' comes from 'scrivener', meaning someone who writes things down. In the 1700s, 'screevers' drew images of current events, for people who couldn't read or write. Sometimes they added comments or poems. By 1890, the number of people living in total poverty had risen greatly, and at least 500 pavement artists were making a living in London.

Modern pavement artists still use chalk but their work has become a respected form of art. Festivals are now held to celebrate and promote pavement art around the world. In some parts of the world it is known as 'street painting'.

One of the largest street-painting festivals is held every year in Florida, USA. It attracts 100,000 visitors and includes over 250 works of pavement art by more than 400 artists.

On 19 and 20 June 2010, a total of 171 drawings by various artists were displayed at the Pasadena Chalk Festival in Pasadena, USA, breaking the Guinness World Record for the largest display of chalk pavement art.

ON YOUR MARKS

a. What else are pavement artists called?

b. Why do you think there were so many pavement artists in London in 1890?

c. How did pavement artists make a living?

GET SET

a. How old might the term 'screever' actually be?

b. What does the word 'promote' mean?

c. What evidence suggests that pavement art is now a respected art form?

GO FOR GOLD!

a. What is another name for pavement art?

b. How do you think people who couldn't read benefited from pavement art?

c. Why do you think modern pavement artists need to create art that attracts people?

BEYOND THE RECORD

'Pavement art is the same thing as graffiti.' Discuss this statement with a partner or small group. Draw a table with two columns. Write ideas for why this might be true in one column, and why it might not be true in the other.

MOST TREES PLANTED SIMULTANEOUSLY

Our World Encyclopedia

Deforestation

Deforestation is the clearing of rainforests, for logging, farming or mining. Large areas of forest are often burned, creating greenhouse gases that lead to climate change. Clearing of the forest destroys animal habitats.

When trees are removed from areas of forest, the fertile topsoil is exposed and washed away by rain. When the topsoil is gone, any water from further rainfall runs off the land quickly, rather than being absorbed. This can lead to flooding and landslides.

Forests

In the Philippines (a large group of islands in South East Asia) more than 70% of the forest has been lost because of illegal logging and the spread of farming and mining.

The El Verde project in Camarines Sur was set up to try to reverse the effects of deforestation in the Philippines by planting more trees.

As part of the project, and to draw attention to it, El Verde broke the Guinness World Record for the most trees planted simultaneously on 23 February 2011, when 6,893 people planted 64,096 trees.

The project was actively supported by the Governor of the area, who encouraged everyone to get involved. He wanted to show the world 'If Camarines Sur can do it, everyone can!'

ON YOUR MARKS

a. What is deforestation?

b. What are three effects of deforestation?

c. How did the Governor of the area help support the El Verde project?

GET SET

a. What are the Philippines?

b. Give three reasons why rainforests are cleared.

c. What is 'illegal logging'?

GO FOR GOLD!

a. Who said: 'If Camarines Sur can do it, everyone can!'?

b. What does 'fertile' mean?

c. What do the organisers of the El Verde project hope to achieve?

BEYOND THE RECORD

Write a letter to the El Verde project organisers to congratulate them on their Guinness World Record.

LARGEST PLAYING CARD STRUCTURE

 www.playingcardstructures/bryan-berg

Bryan Berg: Card stacker

About

Born:
21 March 1974, Spirit Lake, Iowa, USA

Qualifications:
Professional Degree in Architecture, Iowa State University, USA, 1997
Master's Degree in Design Studies, Harvard Graduate School of Design, 2004

Occupation:
Professional card stacker

Lives in:
Santa Fé, New Mexico, USA

Published works:
Stacking the Deck by Bryan Berg

Future plans:
Waiting for the perfect place to build (and demolish) a card tower over 30 m tall

Achievements

1982
Aged eight, Bryan was introduced to card stacking by his grandfather.

1992
First broke the Guinness World Record for tallest house of freestanding playing cards at the age of 17. (He has continuously held the record to date.)

1994
First card-stacking event abroad, in Japan. Built a card shrine for a TV show.

2004
Guinness World Records created a new category to recognise Berg's work: largest house of freestanding playing cards.

2010
Set a new Guinness World Record on 10 March for the largest playing card structure, at the Venetian Casino, Macao, China. The structure was 10.39 m long, 3.54 m wide and 2.88 m high.

Projects

Silverstar Casino, South Africa

Beijing Olympic Village

Holiday Inn Key-card hotel

Cinderella's Castle, Disney World

New York City Skyline

Dallas City Skyline

San Francisco Opera House

ON YOUR MARKS

a. Who first introduced Bryan to card stacking?

b. How does Bryan earn a living?

c. What might you find out by clicking on the link to 'Stacking the Deck by Bryan Berg'?

GET SET

a. Where was Bryan Berg born?

b. Has anyone else broken the record for tallest house of freestanding playing cards? How do you know?

c. What might you find out by clicking on 'Cinderella's Castle, Disney World'?

GO FOR GOLD!

a. What does Bryan want to build in the future?

b. What sort of text is this web page? Explain how you know.

c. How do Bryan's qualifications help him create card buildings?

BEYOND THE RECORD

Change the information in the web page into a timeline. Think carefully about how far apart each milestone is placed.

LONGEST NOSE ON A LIVING PERSON

Your nose

The nose plays a more important role than just how you look.

Smelling
Your nose contains special cells that help you smell as air enters your nose.

Breathing
Your nose plays a vital part in helping you take air into your body to circulate around your lungs. When you breathe in, tiny hairs inside your nose filter out impurities from the air.

Tasting
Your nose helps you taste your food.

Try this!
Eat a piece of something tasty. Pinch your nose and have another piece. Can you taste the difference?

Famous noses

- Cyrano de Bergerac, a French author, was more famous for his nose than for the plays he wrote. Stories based on his life always portray him with an overly large nose, which people would travel a long way to see.

- Pinocchio is a fictional character from a children's novel, *The Adventures of Pinocchio*, by Carlo Collodi, written in 1883, and made more famous by the Disney cartoon. Pinocchio is a wooden puppet whose nose grows longer every time he tells a lie.

- The longest nose on a living person measures 8.8 cm from the bridge to the tip, and belongs to Mehmet Ozyurek from Turkey. It was measured on the set of *Lo Show dei Record* in Rome, Italy, on 18 March 2010.

Encyclopedia of the Human Body **87**

ON YOUR MARKS

a. How does your nose stop you from breathing in impurities in the air?

b. Explain the meaning of the phrase 'fictional character'.

c. Why do you think the Disney cartoon made Pinocchio famous?

GET SET

a. What is inside your nose that helps you smell things?

b. Why does your nose need to filter out impurities?

c. Of the three things your nose does, which do you think is the most important? Why?

GO FOR GOLD!

a. Which person's nose would people travel a long way to see?

b. What are 'impurities'?

c. If you had to have one of the three famous noses from the text, which would you choose? Why?

BEYOND THE RECORD

Use two sources to find out about your other senses: hearing, sight and touch. Create a poster to present this information to a younger age group.

LONGEST DANCING DRAGON

The legend of the Dragon King

Long ago in China, the Dragon King felt an awful pain in his side. He tried everything he could to make the pain go away. He took all the medicine he could find but the pain stayed. Desperate for some relief, he changed into human form and went to see a Chinese doctor.

The doctor examined him and soon exclaimed, 'You are not human!'

The dragon knew he couldn't pretend anymore so he turned back into his true form. The poor doctor was terrified to see a real dragon in his surgery, but he was a kind and brave man and hated to see any creature in such pain. So he continued to treat the Dragon King and soon the pain eased.

The Dragon King was so grateful he decided to help the doctor in return.

'Tell your people to dance in the form of a dragon and you will be granted good luck, fine weather and good harvests every time,' he told the doctor.

So the people danced in long lines, holding aloft a cloth dragon on high poles, whenever they needed good fortune – and they still do to this day.

Did you know...?

The longest dancing dragon was 5,056 m and was made according to old traditions for the opening ceremony of the 25th Luoyang Peony Festival of Henan Province, China, on 10 April 2007.

Legends and Myths **103**

ON YOUR MARKS

a. Where was the Dragon King's pain?

b. Why did the Dragon King change back into his 'true form'?

c. Why do you think the doctor was terrified by the Dragon King?

GET SET

a. Where is the story set?

b. Why did the Dragon King choose to be in human form to see the doctor?

c. Why was the Dragon King grateful?

GO FOR GOLD!

a. What three benefits would come to the people by performing a dragon dance?

b. What sort of story is this? Find evidence in the text.

c. Why do you think a dragon dance was performed at the opening of the 25th Luoyang Peony Festival?

BEYOND THE RECORD

What do people in different parts of the world do to bring themselves luck? Use three different sources to find out. Do you – or does anyone you know – ever do anything to try to bring good luck for special events or activities?

Magic tricks

ESCAPOLOGY

Escapology is the art of escaping. The escapologist is restrained in some way and escapes without anyone knowing how he or she did it.

An element of danger – such as being in a tank of water or hanging upside down from a crane – is often used to keep the audience 'on the edge of their seats'. Harry Houdini was a famous escapologist who performed these sorts of dangerous tricks.

Escapologists can escape from all kinds of situations and from props including:

- handcuffs
- ropes and chains
- straitjackets
- boxes, crates and cabinets.

Tricks with handcuffs

One record-breaking escapology trick consisted of not one pair of handcuffs but *three* pairs! To make it even more difficult, the trick was performed under water. Zdeněk Bradáč from the Czech Republic broke the Guinness World Record for the fastest time to escape from three handcuffs underwater. It took him just 38.69 seconds to escape in Jablonec nad Nisou, on 9 September 2009. Mr Bradáč also holds the record for the fastest handcuff escape (1.66 seconds).

Circus Skills 35

ON YOUR MARKS

a. Who was Harry Houdini?

b. Why would escaping from restraints while being in a tank of water be dangerous?

c. Why do escapologists use different props and situations in their performances?

GET SET

a. As well as using three sets of handcuffs, what made Zdeněk Bradáč's escape even more difficult?

b. Why would an element of danger keep the audience 'on the edge of their seats'?

c. Why is the word 'three' written in italics?

GO FOR GOLD!

a. What other record is held by Zdeněk Bradáč?

b. What does the phrase 'on the edge of their seats' mean?

c. Why does the text use bullet points for some of the information?

BEYOND THE RECORD

Use three different sources to find out about Harry Houdini and what made him famous. Write and illustrate a short biography of him.

MOST BALLET DANCERS EN POINTE

Last May, I went to Orlando in Florida, USA, to stay with my cousin. She is a dancer and goes to a cool school called Dr Phillips High School Dance Magnet. As well as normal school stuff, they do all sorts of dance.

While I was visiting, students at the school were attempting a new Guinness World Record for the most ballet dancers en pointe at the same time. 'En pointe' is French. It means on the very tip of your toes. I had just started learning pointe work at my own ballet classes, so my cousin said I could join in. We all went to the Orange County Convention Center (that's how *they* spell it) on 22 May 2011. Dancers from the Orlando Ballet were there. Wow!

First there were some performances, then 250 dancers joined in the attempt. It wasn't easy — you had to stay en pointe for a whole minute! I fell off and was discounted, and I wasn't the only one. In the end, 245 dancers kept en pointe and so they set a new Guinness World Record.

I was sad to fall off, but at least I can say my cousin is a Guinness World Record holder!

ON YOUR MARKS

a. What does 'en pointe' mean?

b. In which sort of dancing would you dance en pointe?

c. Why does the author say that the Dr Phillips High School Dance Magnet is 'cool'?

GET SET

a. Where was the record attempt held?

b. How many people failed to stay en pointe for a minute?

c. Who is the author talking about when she says 'that's how *they* spell it'?

GO FOR GOLD!

a. What happened just before the record attempt?

b. Why was the author allowed to join in the record attempt?

c. How did the author feel to be among dancers from the Orlando Ballet?

BEYOND THE RECORD

Find out about pointe ballet shoes using books or the internet. Create a list of good and bad features about dancing en pointe. What is your opinion about dancing en pointe?

LARGEST CHOPSTICKS

Osaka

Osaka is Japan's third largest city. It has a population of 2.5 million. It combines historical and cultural attractions with the delights of a modern Japanese city.

Historical attractions

Sumiyoshi Taisha
Founded in the 3rd century, this is the most famous of the 2,000 Sumiyoshi shrines in Japan.

Osaka Castle
The castle was built in 1583, destroyed in 1615, rebuilt in the 1620s and then burned down after a lightning strike in 1665. The current castle tower was rebuilt in 1931.

Shitennoji Temple
Shitennoji is one of Japan's oldest temples. Entry to the outer grounds is free. A five-storey pagoda, designed in the 6th century, stands in the inner courtyard.

Bunraku Theatre
The National Bunraku Theatre is one of the few places in Japan where you can see the traditional Japanese puppet theatre today. English-language headphones are available.

Modern attractions

Osaka Aquarium
Osaka's spectacular aquarium displays a range of different Pacific Ocean species. Tours begin on the 8th floor and spiral down around a central tank, which houses the main attraction – a whale shark.

On 22 March 2009 Osaka was host to a Guinness World Record. The Wakasa Chopsticks Industry Cooperative manufactured the largest set of chopsticks, measuring 8.4 m long. It took them five months to complete the chopsticks.

45

ON YOUR MARKS

a. On which date was Osaka host to a Guinness World Record?

b. What is the natural habitat of the different species found in the Osaka Aquarium?

c. Which attraction can no longer be seen?

GET SET

a. Who manufactured the largest set of chopsticks?

b. Which is the oldest attraction in Osaka?

c. What would you need to do in order to visit the five-storey pagoda in the Shitennoji Temple?

GO FOR GOLD!

a. How long did it take to complete the largest set of chopsticks?

b. What makes the National Bunraku Theatre so important to Japan?

c. Why are English-language headphones provided in the National Bunraku Theatre?

BEYOND THE RECORD

What attractions are there for visitors to the place where you live? Create your own guide to the area. Think about the use of headings, bullet points and pictures to make the information clear for a visitor.

Herentals Herald Sunday 6 July 2003

HERENTALS HOSPITAL: BREAKING RECORDS, NOT BONES!

If you were in the main square of Herentals yesterday, you may have seen a record-breaking event. It was organised by Belgium's Herentals Hospital to celebrate its 750th anniversary. A team of 10 people broke the Guinness World Record for the most plaster casts applied in an hour, by applying 825 forearm plaster casts. That's 82.5 casts per person – an average of 43.6 seconds per cast!

The team applied traditional plaster casts. These are made with a soft layer of bandage against the skin and a hard, heavy covering – usually plaster of Paris. (More modern types of plaster cast are made with light strips of fibreglass bandage instead of plaster.) A plaster cast is often used to hold broken bones still so that they can heal properly.

The hospital staff advised anyone who thinks they may have broken a bone to seek medical advice. They also had useful tips for helping broken bones mend.

1. Rest for the first 12 hours with your arm or leg raised on a pillow. This will help any swelling go down.
2. Do not get the plaster cast wet. If you do, the plaster cast will soften.
3. Do not poke anything down your plaster cast as you may damage your skin and get a nasty sore.

by **SONIA SAHIL**

ON YOUR MARKS

a. How many people had a plaster cast applied to their forearm to set the record?

b. When does someone need a plaster cast?

c. Why does 'Paris' have a capital letter?

GET SET

a. On average, how many casts did one person apply to set the record?

b. Why might a modern plaster cast be preferred to a traditional plaster of Paris cast?

c. Why might someone want to poke something down a plaster cast?

GO FOR GOLD!

a. On average, how quickly did each person apply a single plaster cast?

b. What do both types of plaster cast have in common?

c. How might a softened plaster cast be a problem?

BEYOND THE RECORD

Discuss what you should do if a friend falls and is hurt while out playing. Write a leaflet to explain this for younger children. Think about the best way to present information to your readers. How will you use headings, pictures and colour to do this?

51

Our World Encyclopedia

The Sioux

Tribes

The Sioux Nation consists of seven different tribes in the Great Plains of North America. In ancient times, the Sioux tribes were nomadic people who travelled around and traded with each other. Family life, children and horses were very important to them.

Sioux women were in charge of their camps and tents, called tipis. Sioux men were famous for being great horsemen and warriors. The Sioux war bonnet, or headdress, is an image that represents a Sioux warrior. The bonnets were made with the tail feathers of the golden eagle. Each feather had to be earned by an act of bravery. The feathers might be painted with red dye as a reminder of a particular deed. The bonnets were sometimes decorated with ermine, the white winter coat of a North American stoat, and complicated beadwork.

War bonnets were used for ceremonial occasions and not normally worn in battle.

On 19 August 2008, a sculptor called Michel Schmid broke the Guinness World Record for the largest wooden sculpture, in Porrentruy, Switzerland. The sculpture measured 22.92 m in height and depicted the head of a Sioux warrior.

37

ON YOUR MARKS

a. Who broke the Guinness World Record for the largest wooden sculpture in 2008?

b. What does 'nomadic' mean?

c. Why were horses important to the Sioux way of life?

GET SET

a. Where was the Guinness World Record for the largest wooden sculpture broken?

b. What did a Sioux need to do to get feathers for a headdress?

c. Why do you think war bonnets were kept for ceremonial occasions?

GO FOR GOLD!

a. What did the largest wooden sculpture depict?

b. Why might you be surprised to see a Sioux headdress in Switzerland?

c. What would a headdress with lots of eagle feathers say about its owner?

BEYOND THE RECORD

Use the internet to find out more about how Sioux warriors dressed. Draw and label a picture.

www.extremesportingfeats.com/skating/TaigKhris

TAÏG KHRIS

ABOUT

Taïg Khris is a hugely successful <u>extreme sports</u> athlete. As a professional inline skater, he has become a world-famous superstar and has set many records.

Born in <u>Algiers</u> on 27 July 1975, he started skating when he was just six years old. When he was 21, he took up inline skating and hasn't looked back. He has won every major title in the sport.

RECORDS
2010

On May 29 2010, Taïg set the record for the highest inline skate drop into a <u>halfpipe</u> during the <u>M6 Mobile Mega Jump</u> event in Paris, France. He dropped a staggering 12.5 m.

He also broke the Guinness World Record for the highest roller skate jump when he dropped 39.9 m from the first floor of the Eiffel Tower in Paris onto a massive <u>vert ramp</u> below.

2011

Taïg set a new world record for a roller skating jump by leaping 29 m down a long ramp in front of the <u>Sacre Coeur Basilica</u> in Paris.

GLOSSARY

Algiers: the capital city of Algeria, North Africa.

Extreme sports: sports with elements of danger and needing a high level of skill.

Halfpipe: a curved ramp.

M6 Mobile Mega Jump: inline skating event.

Sacre Coeur Basilica: a large Catholic church.

Vert ramp: a type of halfpipe.

Wakeboarding: a water sport where you ride a wakeboard over the surface of water.

TRIVIA

- Height: 181 cm
- Speaks five languages
- Performs street magic
- Plays the piano
- Enjoys snowboarding and <u>wakeboarding</u>

ON YOUR MARKS

a. How old was Taïg Khris when he first started skating?

b. Name one other extreme sport that Taïg does.

c. Why do some terms in the article have definitions?

GET SET

a. Where did Taïg Khris set the record for the highest inline skate drop into a halfpipe?

b. Why is the glossary in alphabetical order?

c. What does the phrase 'hasn't looked back' mean in this web page?

GO FOR GOLD!

a. In which country was Taïg Khris born?

b. Explain the purpose of the section headed 'Trivia'.

c. Why do you think Taïg Khris has become world famous?

BEYOND THE RECORD

Write an extended glossary for the text so that younger children will understand it. What other words or phrases will you include?

READING SKILLS

There are different skills you need to learn when reading texts.

Each AF (assessment focus) describes a different set of reading skills. In this book, you will actively practise and improve your ability to do the following.

AF2:

- Find information in a text.
- Find evidence in a text.

AF3:

- Understand what the writer means but does not tell you directly.

AF4:

- Find patterns in a text.
- Comment on organisation of texts.

AF5:

- Understand why the writer chooses a word.
- Understand why writers sometimes use very short sentences.
- Comment on how a writer uses language for effect.

AF6:

- Identify the writer's purpose.
- Understand the writer's viewpoint and the overall effect of the text.